AF488461

This book is dedicated to you, as you continue your walk with Jesus Christ
don't forget to wear your armor!
Every single piece has been created especially for you to stand tall
against the evil and injustice of this world
and to spread the Word of God to all.
Whenever you are getting dressed for the day and you look in the mirror
and see the Armor of God covering you,
Just know you have already won, and the enemy has been defeated!

EPHESIANS 6:12-17 ERV

Our fight is not against people on earth.

We are fighting against the rulers and authorities
and the powers of this world's darkness.

We are fighting against the spiritual powers of evil
in the heavenly places.

That is why you need to get God's full armor.

Then on the day of evil, you will be able
to stand strong.

And when you have finished the whole fight,
you will still be standing.

So stand strong with the belt of truth tied around
your waist, and on your chest wear the protection
of right living.

On your feet wear the Good News of peace
to help you stand strong.

And also use the shield of faith with which you
can stop all the burning arrows that come
from the Evil One.

Accept God's salvation as your helmet.

And take the sword of the Spirit
that sword is the teaching of God.

WHERE IS YOUR ARMOR?

Inspired by Holy Spirit

Author: Symone Anderson
Illustrator: Larissa Sharina

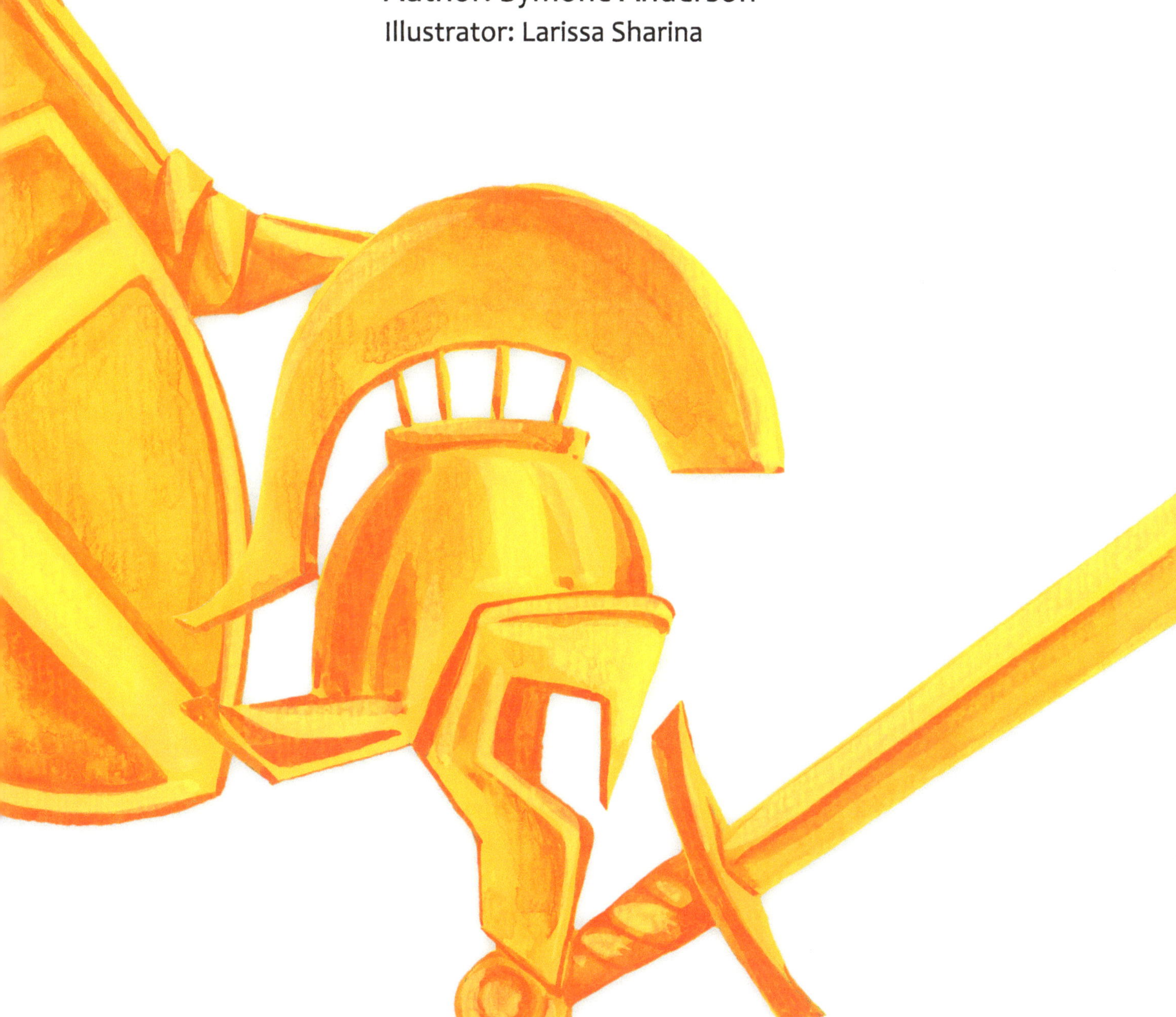

1

Getting dressed and I see
something missing what could it be?

As I began to look and see,
I noticed my BELT OF TRUTH was missing!

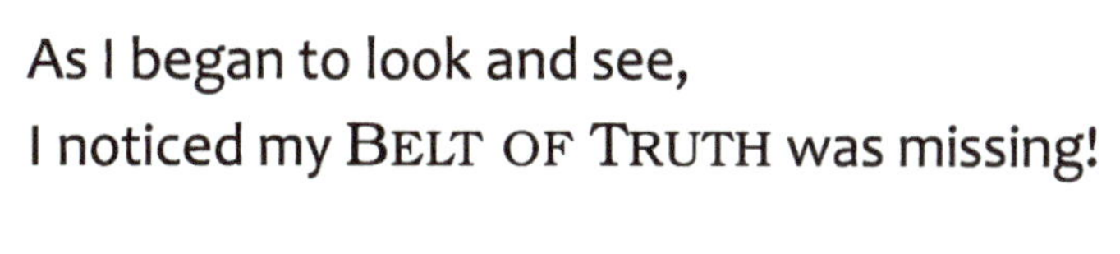

Putting my shirt on and straightening it out
Questioning if I left my BREASTPLATE OF RIGHTEOUSNESS
somewhere near the couch?

After finding my BELT OF TRUTH
and BREASTPLATE OF RIGHTEOUSNESS

6
I realized my SHOES OF PEACE
were completely displaced!

Finally getting ready to leave with most of my things

How could I forget to bring my SHIELD OF FAITH with me?

Wrapping my jacket around my shoulders,
preparing for the outside weather

Nothing can replace my HELMET OF SALVATION;
now where did I last put it?

Arriving to my favorite place
with my armor on and a smile on my face.
Armed with the SWORD OF THE SPIRIT,
prepared to share God's word at any given minute.

12
No matter the day, week or the year,
the pieces of armor I wear
will help me defeat the enemy
and have the victory!

THE ARMOR OF GOD

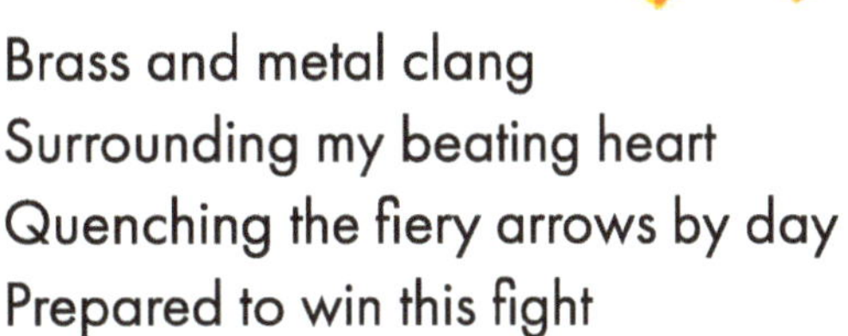

Your words surround me
Protecting me from all sides
Keeping me from the enemy
You made it just for me
Precisely in my size

Brass and metal clang
Surrounding my beating heart
Quenching the fiery arrows by day
Prepared to win this fight

Placing one foot in after another
Steady and firm the steps I take
As I move along
Calm and reassuring are my words
Lovingly expressed through scripture and song

Wide and tall it stands
Shining power and glory
Held with my hands
My scars you see tell my story

Crowning my head, broad and sturdy
Fitting the frame of my face perfectly
Representing a promise
Of life everlasting

Held up high, brightly shining
Sharpened throughout my spiritual journey
Walking in the fullness of my authority
Defeating the fear and unbelief which once captured me.

Prayer of Salvation

I confess that Jesus is Lord
and I believe that you
died on the cross for my sins
and rose from the grave!

I accept you, Jesus Christ as my
Lord and Savior and
I ask you Lord to come
into my heart and show me
how to live for you!

In Jesus name, I pray, Amen!